HER BODY CAN

Katie Crenshaw & Ady Meschke

Illustrated by Li Liu

EAST 26th PUBLISHING

HOUSTON

Her Body Can

Libary of Congress Cataloging-in-Publication data is available
ISBN: 978-0-578-65148-4

Editing, book layout and cover by Krista Huber
Typography is Julius Primary set in size 27

10 9 8 7 6 5 4 3 2 1
First printing edition 2020

East 26th Publishing
Houston, TX

www.east26thpublishing.com

Her body can smile, frown, rest or hustle!

She's oh so much more than brains, bones and muscle.

Her body can wear any color or costume.

On the bus, at the park, on stage, in the classroom.

Her body can play with all friends of each size.

Worth is not measured by the shapes of our thighs.

Her body can choose kale or cake—
Yummy, Yummy!
Food is her fuel and feels good in
her tummy.

Her body can run,

jump, spin and dance.

She's not afraid to give new moves a chance.

Her body can shop
at the stores she likes best

She gets to choose how she wants to dress.

Her body can swim and splash in the pool.

A one-piece or two-piece
will help her stay cool.

Her body can pose
for pictures—Say Cheese!

She'll love looking back at the fun memories.

Her body is BEAUTIFUL—
strong, kind and wise.

All bodies are lovely no matter their size.

Her body can dream
of the places she'll go;

From Paris to London—perhaps Tokyo.

Her body can know that words people say

shouldn't hurt her or change her

or push her away.

Her body can look at herself in the mirror.

She is perfectly perfect. It's never been clearer!

Her body can
go over
and under
and through.

And what
her body can,
darling,
yours can do too.

Dear Reader,

We believe, in the depths of our souls, that all bodies are inherently good, capable and miraculous. As former little girls turned women, we are all too familiar with the limits society tries to set for us and what our culture expects a girl to look like, act like, and be like.

We want to encourage girls from ages 1 to 101 that your body CAN.

Your body's most important job is to carry you—an irreplaceable human being— through your life's journey. As you grow and experience life, it is important that you love your body and yourself with the entirety of your heart.

What your body looks like is irrelevant.

When you connect to your inner self and focus on what you CAN DO, unconditionally loving and honoring your body becomes one of the centerpoints of life.

Always treat your body like it's holding your inner child—who is worthy of respect and adoration no matter what. Whenever you feel like others may be telling you otherwise, just remember: You are amazing and so is your body.

Love, K & A

ABOUT THE AUTHORS

Ady Meschke and Katie Crenshaw are Atlanta-based bloggers and mothers working to spread messages of body positivity and self-love through honest conversations with their followers.

Ady is an award-winning travel blogger for Verbal Gold Blog, and a body-inclusive activewear mogul who has been featured in national publications such as Shape and The Today Show. To learn more about Ady and her mission, follow her on Instagram @verbalgoldblog or visit her website at www.verbalgoldblog.com

Katie is a nationally recognized body-positivity and mental health spokesperson who has been featured on Good Morning America, CNN and Inside Edition, and is the 2020 spokesperson for The Blue Dot Project. To learn more about Katie and her mission, follow her on Instagram @katiemcrenshaw or visit her website at www.katiecrenshaw.com

Made in the USA
Monee, IL
06 March 2020